LAUGH OUT LOUD!
THE JOLLY JUNGLE
JOKE BOOK

Sean Connolly

WINDMILL
BOOKS

New York

Published in 2013 by Windmill Books, An Imprint of Rosen Publishing
29 East 21st Street, New York, NY 10010

First Edition

Editor: Joe Harris
Illustrations: Adam Clay (cover) and Dynamo Design (interiors)
Layout Design: Notion Design

Library of Congress Cataloging-in-Publication Data

Connolly, Sean, 1956–
   The jolly jungle joke book / by Sean Connolly. — 1st ed.
      p. cm. — (Laugh out loud)
   Includes index.
   ISBN 978-1-61533-646-3 (library binding) — ISBN 978-1-61533-658-6 (pbk.) —
   ISBN 978-1-61533-659-3 (6-pack)
   1. Jungles—Juvenile humor. 2. Jungle animals—Juvenile humor. 3. Riddles, Juvenile. I. Title.
   PN6231.J86C55 2013
   808.88'2—dc23
                                    2012019526

Printed in China

CPSIA Compliance Information: Batch #AW3102WM: For Further Information contact Windmill Books, New York, New York at 1-866-478-0556
SL002426US

CONTENTS

JOLLY JUNGLE

Why should you never trust a giraffe?
They are always telling tall stories.

Is it a good idea to buy a pet skunk?
Yes, it makes a lot of scents!

What flies through the jungle singing opera?
The Parrots of Penzance.

Teacher: What do you think a pair of alligator shoes would cost?
Pupil: That would depend on the size of your alligator's feet!

Why do elephants paint their toenails red?
So they can hide in cherry trees!

JOLLY JUNGLE

What were Tarzan's
last words?
"Who greased the
v-i-i-i-i-i-i-i-i-n-e?"

Knock, knock!
Who's there?
Giraffe.
Giraffe who?
Giraffe to ask me
that stupid question?

How do you make orange crush?
Get an elephant to jump up and down in the fruit and
vegetable aisle!

How do hippos commute?
By hippopotabus.

Teacher: Define "polygon."
Pupil: A missing parrot!

What do you get if you cross a parrot with a centipede?
A walkie talkie.

Why were the sweet potatoes playing jazz music?
They were having a yam session.

What do you call a lion with no eyes?
Lon!

Why should you never surprise a parrot perching on a doorknob?
Because it might fly off the handle!

What happened when the skunk fell in the river?
It stank all the way to the bottom.

JOLLY JUNGLE

How can you tell the difference between an African elephant and an Indian elephant?
Look at their passports!

What do elephants take to help them sleep?
Trunkquilizers!

Spotted in the jungle library:
"Why Giant Snails Get Tired" by Michelle Sevy.

Who won the giraffe race?
Nobody knows— the competitors were neck and neck!

What's gray, weighs five tons, and bounces?
A bungee-jumping elephant.

What sort of dancing will elephants do in your front room?
Break dancing!

Why can't I get the king of the jungle on the telephone?
Because the lion is busy!

Teacher: Have you written your essay on big cats?
Pupil: I thought it would be safer to use paper!

What do you call a lion with toothache?
Rory!

What do you call a hippo
that always claims to be sick?
A hippochondriac.

Why did the firefly keep crashing? He wasn't very bright.

What did King Kong say when he was told that his sister had had a baby? Well, I'll be a monkey's uncle!

What do you call a show full of lions? The mane event.

Why do birds of paradise have such amazing plumage? They pay attention to detail.

Who is in charge of the stick insects? The branch manager!

Which type of jungle birds prefer to live underground?
Mynahs.

How do you get into the jungle monastery?
With a monk-key.

How does a lion like his steak?
Medium roar.

Why did the chameleon go to the doctor?
He was feeling a little off-color.

How did the chameleon do in his pilot's test?
He passed with flying colors.

JOLLY JUNGLE

What do you call a fashionable big cat?
A dandy lion.

What do you get if you cross a gorilla with a porcupine?
A seat on the bus!

How do you fix a broken chimp?
With a monkey wrench!

What do you get if you cross a tiger and a sheep?
A striped sweater.

What do you get if you cross a snake with a kangaroo?
A jump rope.

Knock, knock!
Who's there?
Orange!
Orange who?
Orange you glad to see me?

Why did King Kong climb up the side of the Empire State Building?
The elevator was broken.

Baby snake: Dad, are we poisonous?
Dad snake: No, son, why do you ask?
Baby snake: I've just bitten my tongue!

What do you call an alligator private eye?
An investi-gator.

What do you get if you cross a tarantula with a rose?
We're not sure, but don't try smelling it!

Why don't bananas sunbathe?
Because they would peel.

What happens if you cross a hummingbird with a doorbell?
You get a humdinger.

What does the lemur do every evening?
He curls up with his favorite tail.

What do chimps learn in first grade?
The ape-B-C's.

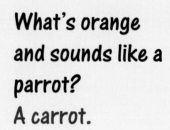

Why does a
frog have more
lives than a cat?
Because it croaks
every night.

What do ape attorneys
study in college?
The law of the jungle.

What's orange
and sounds like a
parrot?
A carrot.

Is it hard to spot a leopard?
Not at all—they come that way!

What do toucans sing at Christmas?
Jungle Bells.

JOLLY JUNGLE

What advice did the parrot give to the toucan?
Talk is cheep.

What do monkeys wear when they cook?
Ape-rons.

How did the monkey get down the stairs?
It slid down the banana-ster.

What did the snake give his date when he dropped
her off?
He gave her a good-night hiss.

Why did the leopard
refuse to take
a bath?
Because he
didn't want
to become
spotless.

What language do oranges speak?
Mandarin.

Why should you never tell a giraffe a secret?
Because you could fall off his neck as you whisper in his ear.

What did Tarzan tell his son?
"Be careful—it's a jungle out there."

What's sweet and crunchy and swings through the trees?
A meringue-utan.

What's worse than a crocodile with a toothache?
A centipede with athlete's foot.

What is a gorilla's favorite ice-cream flavor?
Chocolate chimp.

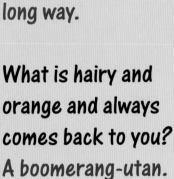

Why do giraffes have small appetites?
Because a little goes a long way.

What is hairy and orange and always comes back to you?
A boomerang-utan.

What happens if you upset a cannibal?
You get into hot water.

What is gray, has huge wings, and gives money to elephants?
The tusk fairy.

Which animals were the last to leave Noah's Ark? The elephants—they had to pack their trunks.

Which U.S. president was voted the all-time favorite by a gorilla convention? Hairy Truman.

What happens if you cross an elephant and a canary? You get a very messy cage.

Why didn't the elephant buy a sports car? It had no trunk space.

What's the most dangerous animal in your backyard? The clothes-lion.

JOLLY JUNGLE

What do you call an exploding ape?
A ba-BOOM!

What did the banana say to the gorilla?
Nothing, bananas can't talk!

What do you get if you cross a snake with a pig?
A boar constrictor.

What do you get when you cross an
elephant with a kangaroo?
Big holes all over Australia.

Why did the
leopard eat the
tightrope
walker?
He wanted a
balanced diet.

JOLLY JUNGLE

Why did the elephant do so well in school?
He had so much gray matter.

What's the best time to buy parakeets?
When they're going cheep.

How do you make an elephant fly?
Start with a three-foot zipper.

Why does Tarzan shout so loudly?
Because it hurts when he pounds his chest.

What do you call two rhinos on a bicycle?
Optimistic.

Teacher: They say time flies like an arrow.
Pupil: Yes, but fruit flies like a banana.

What would you get if a python slipped into a tuba?
A snake in the brass.

What has 99 legs and one eye?
A pirate centipede.

What has three trunks, two tails, and six feet?
An elephant with spare parts.

Why couldn't the butterfly go to the dance?
Because it was a moth ball.

What sort of animal is big, gray, and wears flowers in its hair?
A hippy-potamus.

What is smarter than a talking parrot?
A spelling bee.

What do you give a gorilla that's going to throw up?
Plenty of room!

What did the queen bee say to her nosy next door neighbor?
Mind your own bees' nest.

What is a snake's favorite class at school?
Hisssstory.

JOLLY JUNGLE

Why do elephants never forget?
Because no one ever tells them anything.

What do you get if you cross a parakeet with a
lawn mower?
Shredded tweet.

Why are anteaters so healthy?
Because they're full of anty-bodies.

What do wasps do when they build a new nest?
They have a house-swarming party.

Why was the cobra thrown out of the snake club?
Because he wasn't a mamba.

What did the boa constrictor say to his girlfriend?
"I have a crush on you!"

What do you get if you cross a parrot with a shark?
A bird that will talk your ear off.

What did the bee say when it returned to the hive?
"Honey, I'm home."

What happened to the cannibal lion?
He had to swallow his pride.

What should you do if a rhino charges you?
Pay him!

JOLLY JUNGLE

How did the rival apes settle their differences?
With a gorilla war.

What do you get if you cross an elephant with a parrot?
An animal that tells you everything it remembers.

What's black and white and red all over?
A zebra with a sunburn.

Why did the canary refuse to work in a coal mine?
He said it was beneath him.

What did the tiger say when he cut off his tail?
It won't be long now.

What's the medical term for memory loss in parrots?
Polynesia.

What line of work did the parrot take up after it swallowed a clock?
Politics.

What do you call a rabbit that can beat up a lion?
Sir.

Why should you value an elephant's opinion?
Because it carries a lot of weight.

What do you call a snail on a turtle's shell?
A thrill seeker.

JOLLY JUNGLE

Why did the monkey take the banana to the doctor's?
Because it wasn't peeling well.

How do you start a firefly race?
By saying "On your marks, get set, glow!"

Why did the hippo eat a couch and three chairs?
Because he had a suite tooth.

Knock, knock!
Who's there?
Cash!
Cash who?
No thanks, but
I'd love a peanut!

Why did Tarzan
spend so much time
on the golf course?
He was perfecting
his swing.

Where do monkeys pick up juicy gossip?
On the apevine.

How do we know that panthers are religious?
Because they prey on people.

How did the cannibal commit suicide?
He got himself into a real stew.

If a dictionary goes from A to Z, what goes from Z to A?
A zebra.

How do gorillas stay in shape?
They join jungle gyms.

JOLLY JUNGLE

Which jungle animals are terrified of vampires?
Giraffes—they have such long necks!

Where do monkeys go if they lose their tails?
To the retail store.

Why does a flamingo lift up one leg?
Because if it lifted up both legs it would fall over!

What did the ape call his first wife?
His prime mate.

How much does a lion trainer need to know?
More than the lion!

What do
you call a
failed lion tamer?
Claude Bottom!

Why don't farmers grow bananas
any longer?
Because they're long enough already.

How does the veterinarian dentist check the tiger
for cavities?
Very carefully!

How do you measure a cobra?
In inches—they don't have any feet.

First man: "I took my son to the zoo last week."
Second man: "Really? And which cage is he in now?"

JOLLY JUNGLE

What is the difference between a wet day and an
injured tiger?
One pours with rain and the other roars with pain.

Knock, knock!
Who's there?
Toucan.
Toucan who?
Toucan play at that game.

Did you hear about the
snake archer?
He used a boa
and arrow.

Did you hear about
the crocodile
who took up
photography?
He was snap-happy.

Glossary

attorney (uh-TUR-nee) a lawyer hired by a company or person

lemur (LEE-mur) a primate that lives in the forests of Madagascar

meringue (muh-RANG) a sweet dessert made with egg whites

plumage (PLOO-mij) the feathers on a bird

polygon (PAH-lee-gahn) a shape with straight sides, such as a triangle or square

primate (PRY-mayt) a kind of mammal with hands, such as an ape or monkey

tranquilizers (TRAN-kwih-ly-zerz) drugs that are used to make animals fall asleep

Further Reading

Elliott, Rob. *Zoolarious Animal Jokes for Kids*. Ada, MI: Revell, 2012.

Namm, Diane. *Jumpin' Jungle Jokes*. Laugh Along Readers. New York: Sterling Publishing, 2008.

Winter, Judy A. *Jokes about Animals*. Mankato, MN: Capstone Press, 2011.

Index

Websites

For Web resources related to the subject of this book, go to: www.windmillbooks.com/weblinks and select this book's title.